Chelsey Loves To Read

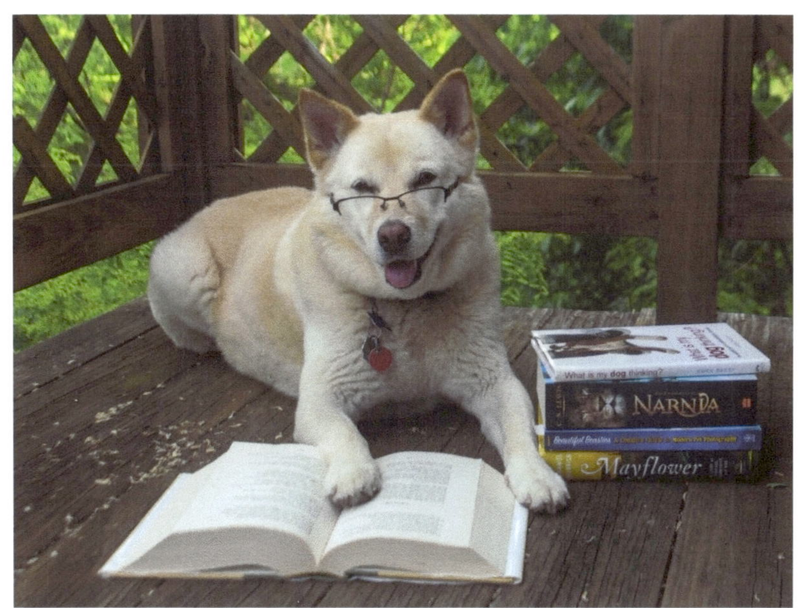

Written and Photos
by: N. K. Hasen

Chelsey Loves To Read

ISBN-13: 978-1-7337994-2-3

In loving memory of Chelsey, my dog, who passed away last year November, 2018.

Hi, my name is Chelsey and I love to read books. My favorite spot to read is on the balcony.

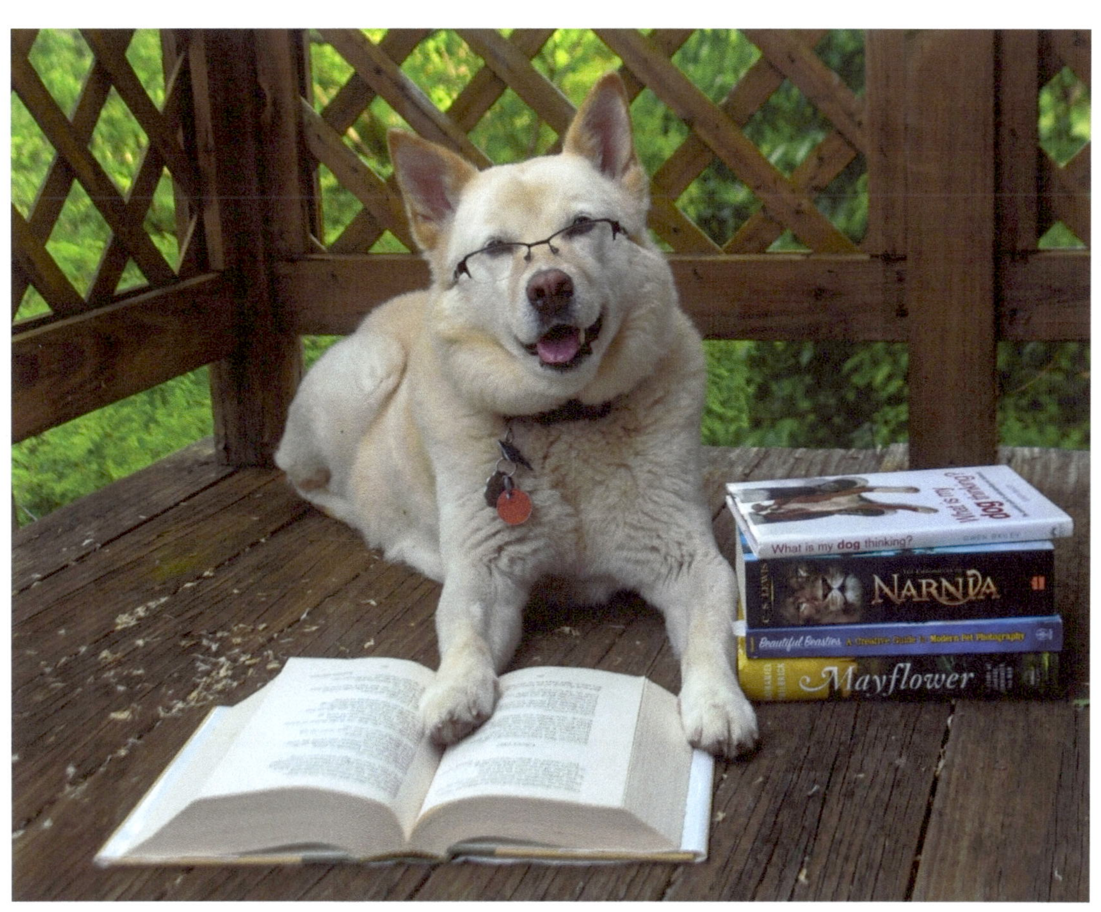
What is my dog thinking?
NARNIA
Beautiful Beasties
Mayflower

I read many different kinds of books. Here is a look at what I am reading now.

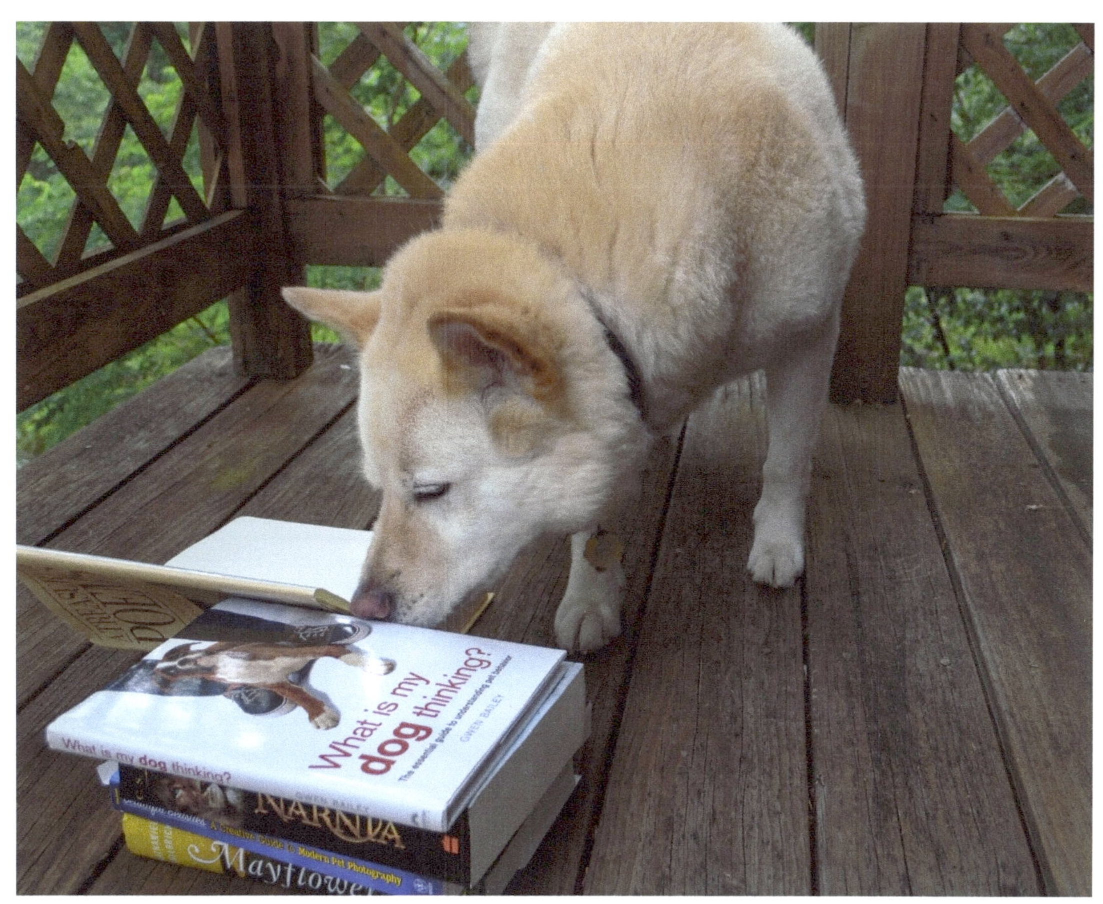

What is my dog thinking?
What is my dog thinking?
The essential guide to understanding pet behavior
dog
NARNIA
A Creative Guide to Modern Pet Photography
Mayflower

I read outside when it is nice and not raining. I wear glasses when reading. It helps to read the words better.

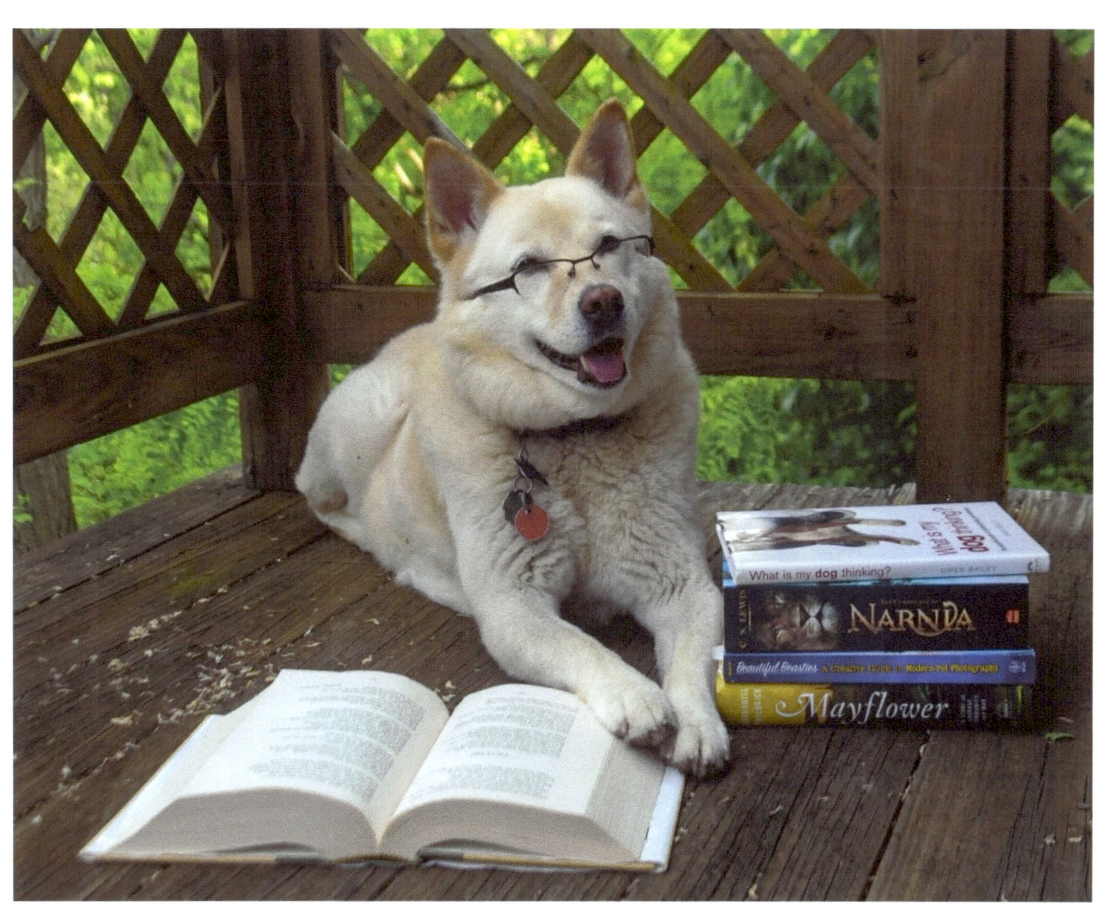
What is my dog thinking?
NARNIA
C. S. LEWIS
Beautiful Beasties A Creative Guide to Modern Pet Photography
Mayflower

I am reading poetry today. There are
many poems in this book. I don't
think I will finish it all today.

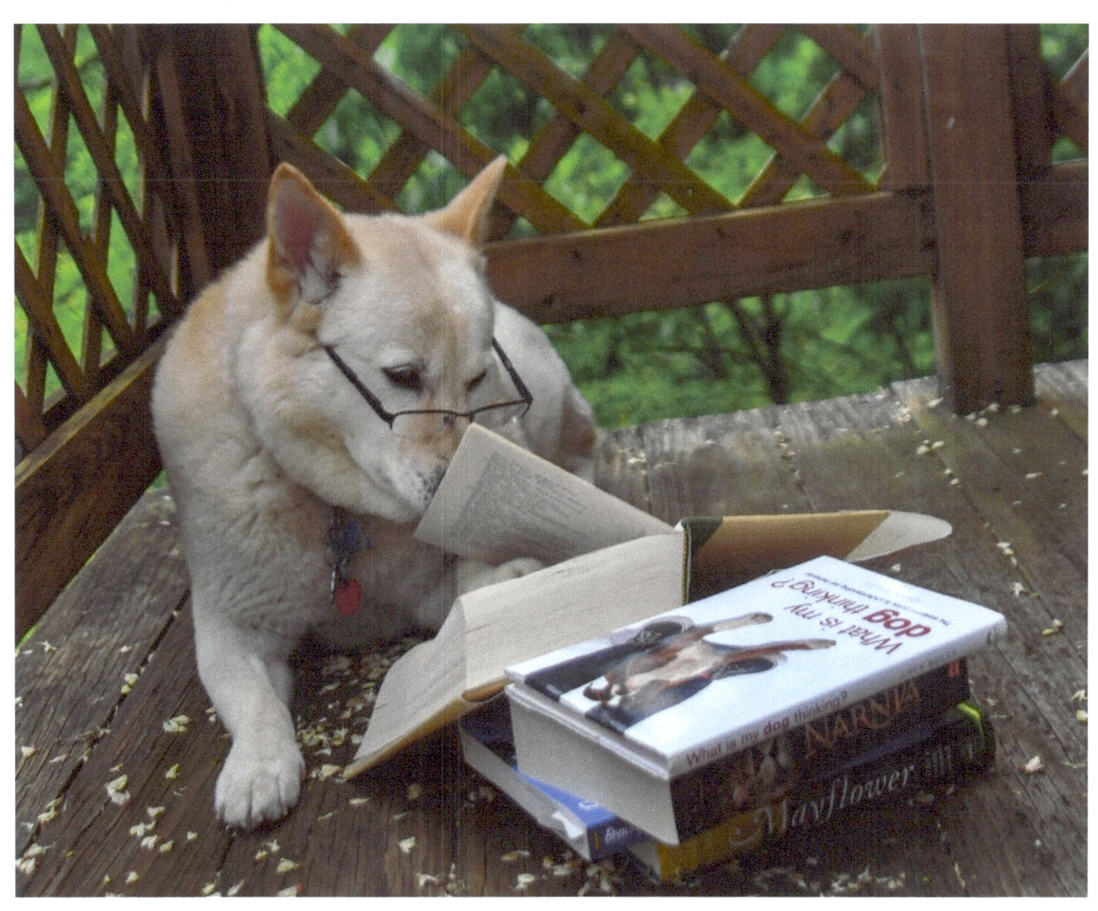

What is my dog thinking?
dog
NARNIA
Mayflower

Here we go! I start to read my poetry book. Some poems are very funny and make me laugh.

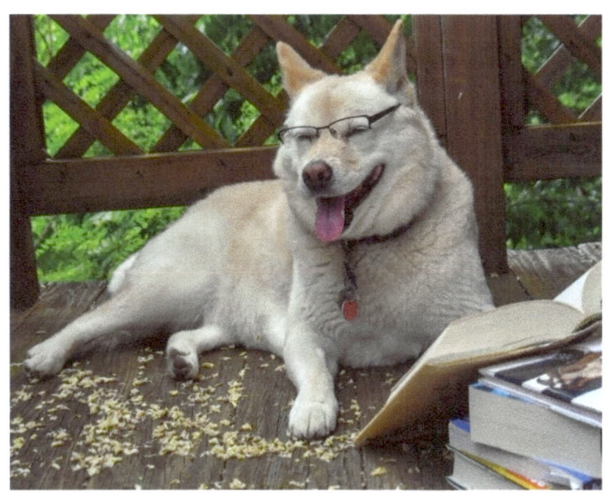

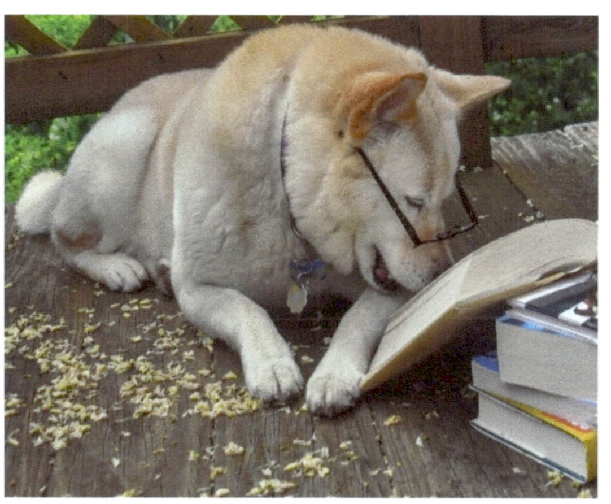

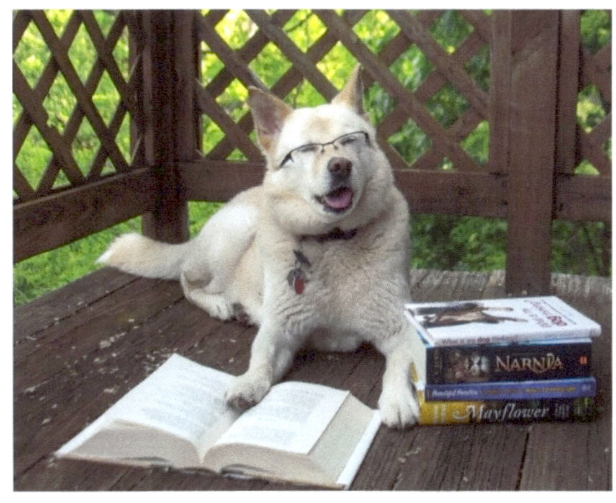

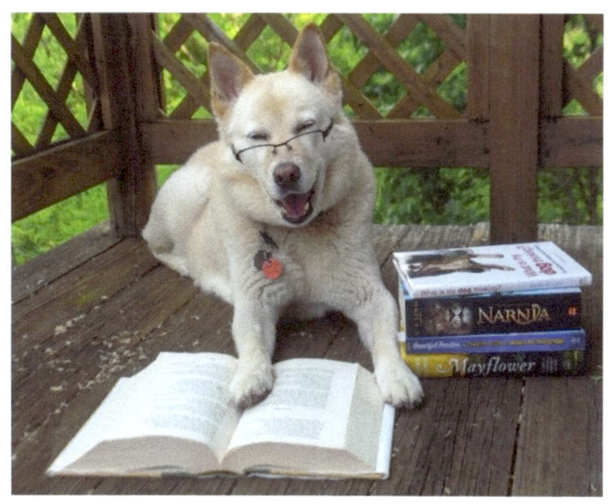

Other poems make me think on their meaning. I lift my snout up and think about them.

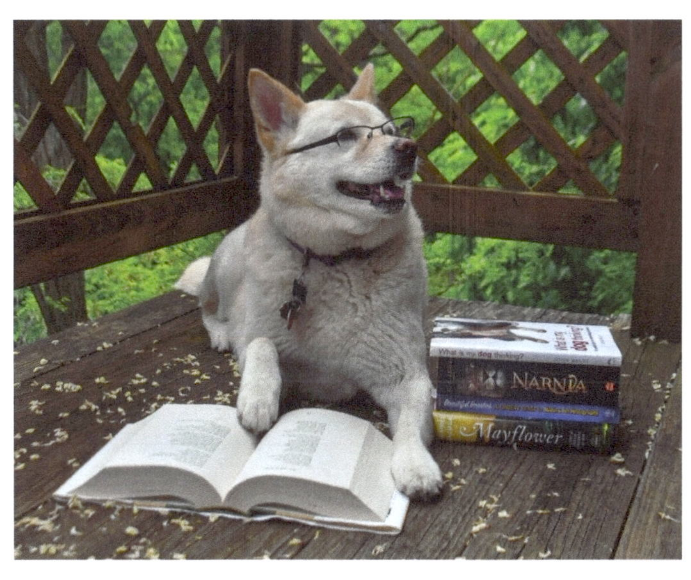

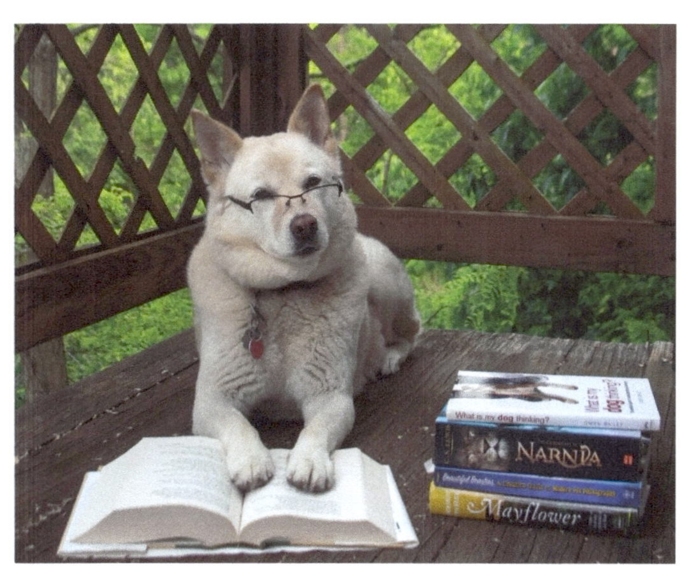

This poem is confusing. I am not sure
what it means. I will ask my owner about
this one later.

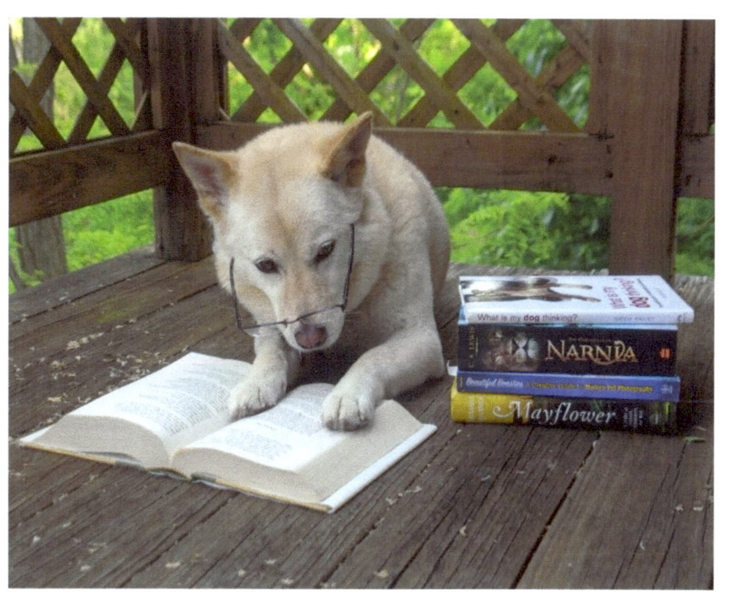

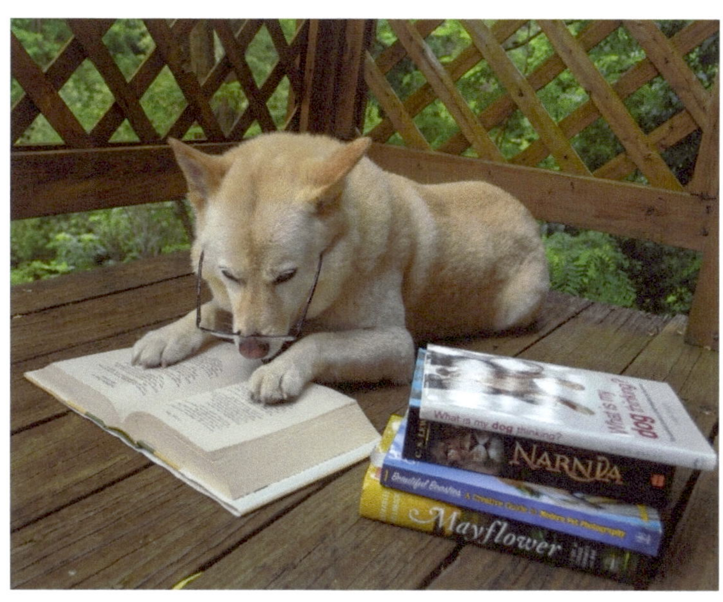

In the middle of reading a poem I hear
something and look up. Just a dog walking
by. I will go back to reading my poetry.

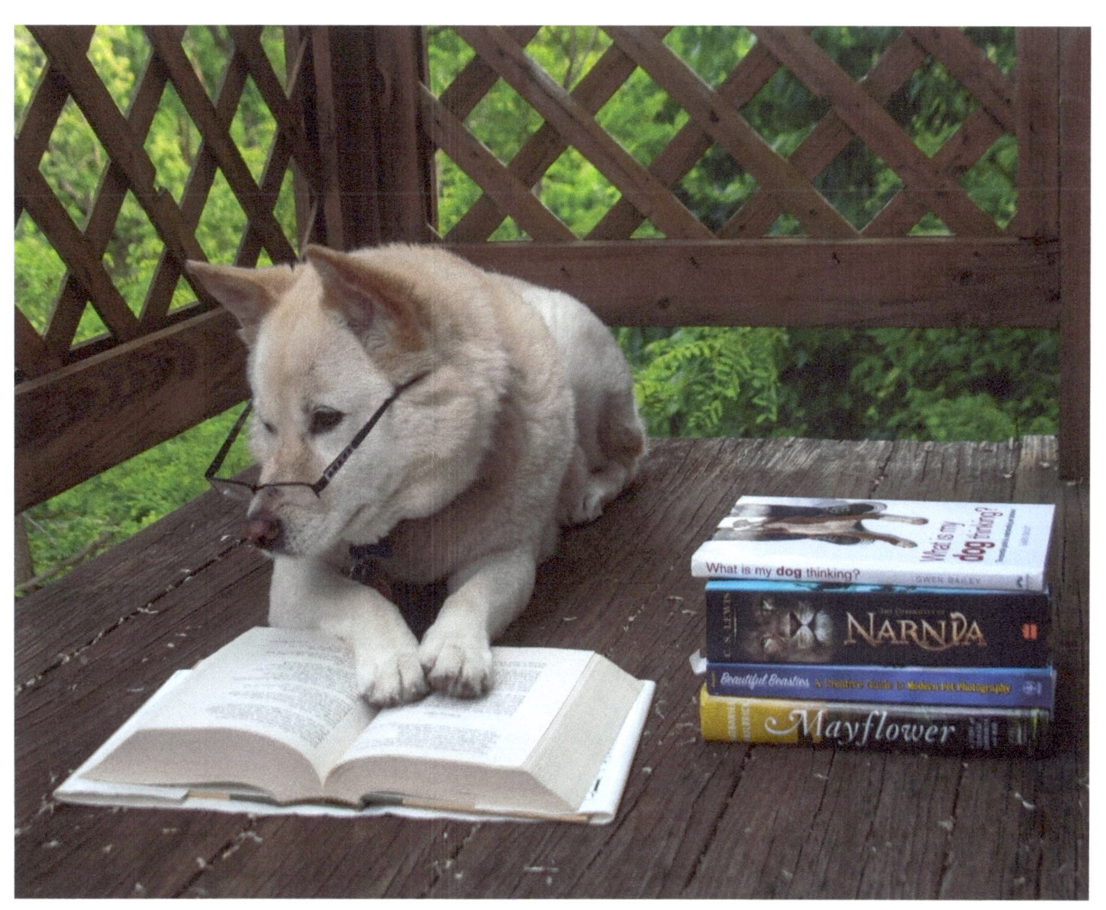

What is my dog thinking?
GWEN BAILEY
THE CHRONICLES OF NARNIA
Beautiful Beasties A Creative Guide to Modern Pet Photography
Mayflower

Right now I am getting into reading my poetry book. This poem I am on now is very interesting and challenging to read.

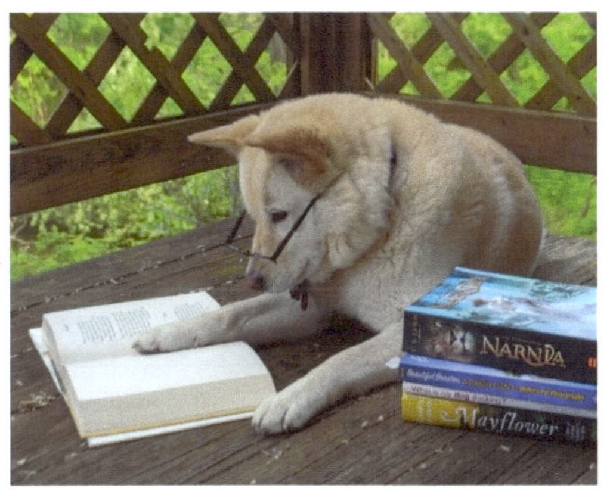 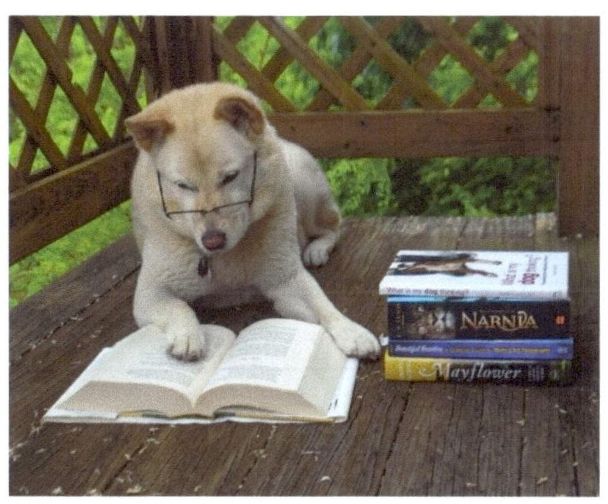

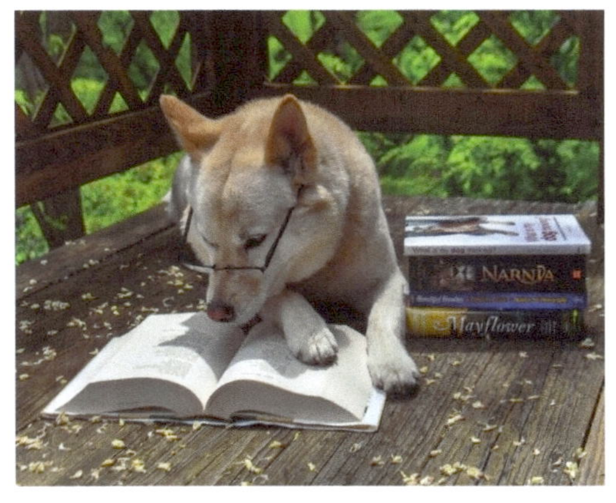 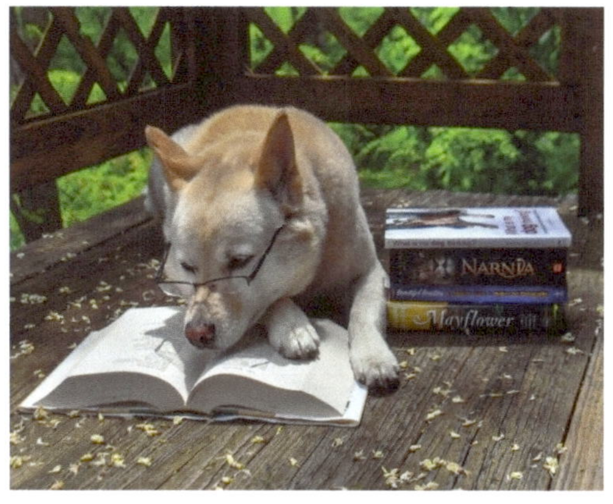

This next poem is very sad and made me
unhappy. I will finish this poem and find
one that makes me happy.

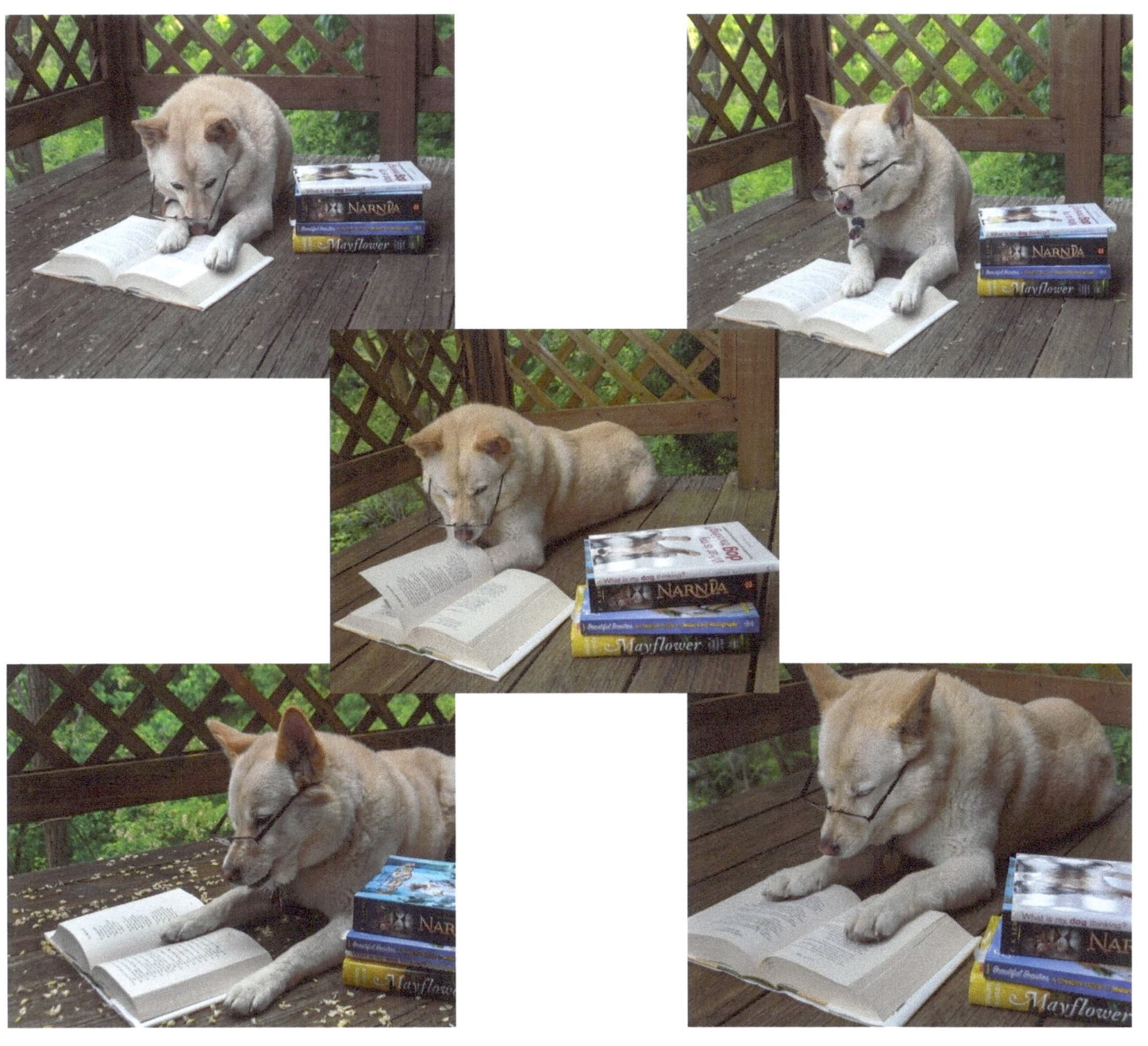

Sometime I change position or change the way I read my books. I decided to prop my poetry book up against the other books I have out.

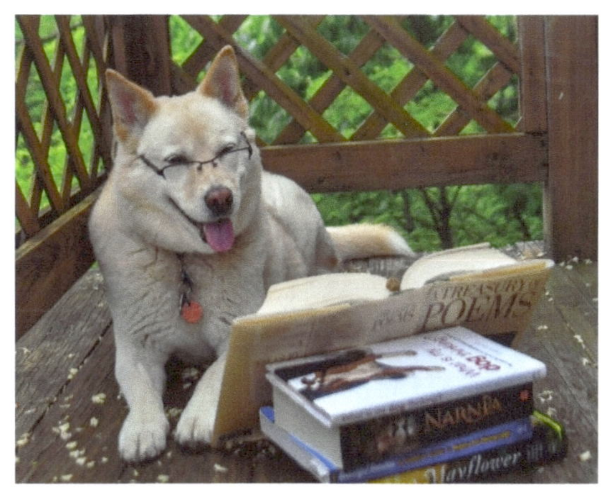
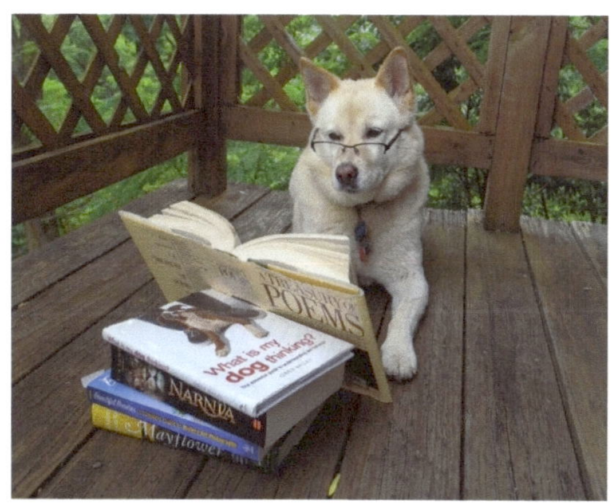
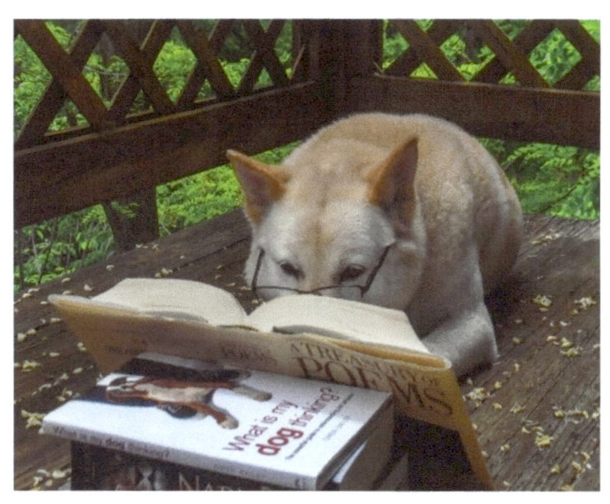
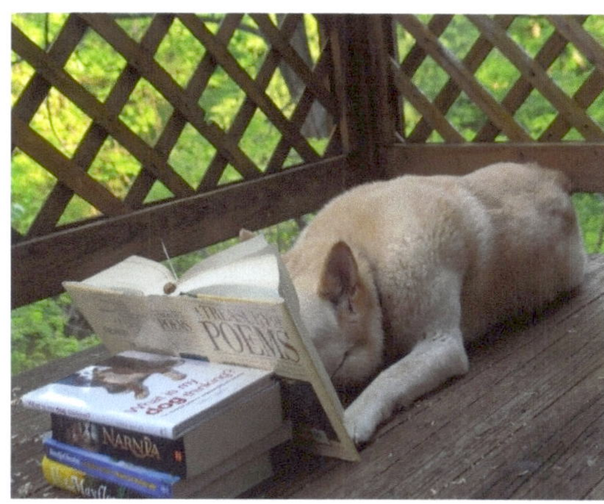

I finished reading my poetry book for now.
I am going to take a look at one more book
before I go for my walk. I'll tell you how
my next book goes another time.

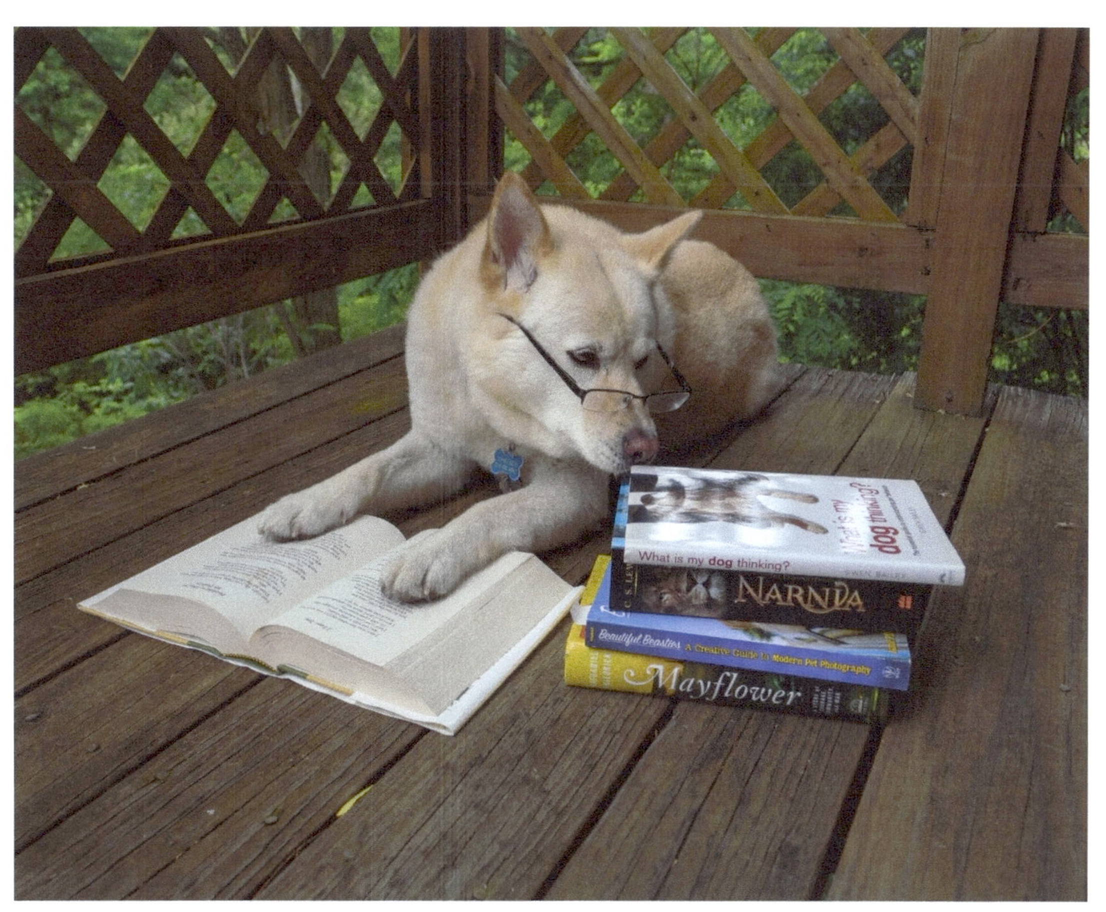

What is my dog thinking?
What is my dog thinking?
NARNIA
C. S. LEWIS
Beautiful Beasties A Creative Guide to Modern Pet Photography
Mayflower

ACKNOWLEDGMENTS

I would like to acknowledge my dog, Chelsey, who was the first dog I owned. She opened my creativity because of her. I found my love of writing and doing photography because of her. She is now in heaven but she continues to give me that creative spark. Thank you, Chelsey for putting up with the photo shoots for these photos. Thank you for the ten years that you gave me and being my best friend. I will always love you, my girl!!

OTHER WORKS

Poetry:

Along a Trodden Path I Travel

Collection of Dog Poetry: Poems About Dog

Something Close At The Roots

30 Poems In 30 Days: April Poetry Challenge

110 Haiku Poems

Ode To Colors

30 Poems In 30 Days: April Poetry Challenge Vol. II

105 Dog Haikus

Collection of Dog Poetry: Poems About Dog Vol. II

Dog Double Elevenie

30 Poems In 30 Days: April Poetry Challenge Vol. III

ABOUT AUTHOR

I am a poet, writer and amateur photographer who lives in Ohio. I have written eleven poetry books. Some of them are two collection of dog poetry, *105 Dog Haikus*, *Something Close At the Roots* and *110 Haiku Poems*. My dog, Chelsey, who recently passed away inspired me in writing poetry and other writings. I have a poetry blog at https://poetryby-hasen.wordpress.com. My other site Dog Photography and Writing is where I combine both my love of photography and writing.

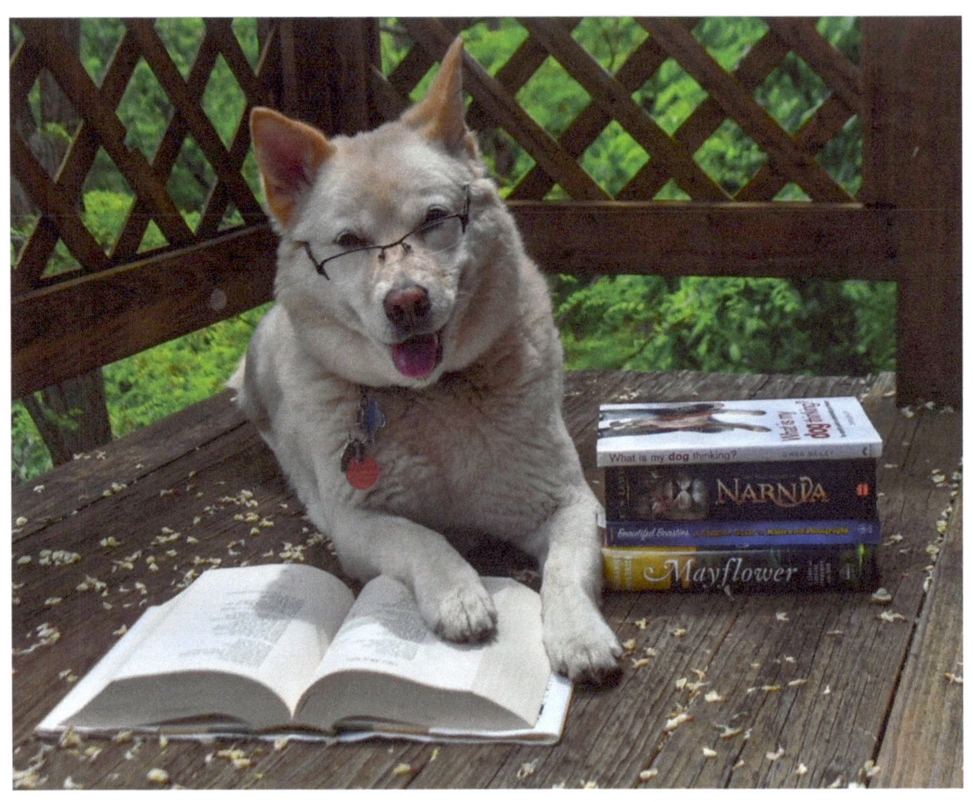

Chelsey

My best friend from:
2008 - 2018